Bygone POLLOKSHAWS

by
George Rountree

ROUND TOLL, POLLOKSHAWS.

The Round Toll, *c*.1910. Road tolls were introduced in 1750 and the round house was built soon after for the toll-keeper who collected the dues. The smaller aperture to the left of the shutter for the big window was probably where travellers on horseback paid their dues. Although tolls had been abandoned in the 1880s, above this aperture there is what looks like a board with a list of charges on it. Coaches and carts would have been attended to in person by the keeper, who had to be on hand to open the barrier. In a situation quite different from the quiet scene seen here, he had to cope with traffic coming from four directions. This postcard view was produced after the tram system had been extended from the terminus at the end of Pollokshaws Road into Cross Street and Harriet Street and on to Rouken Glen.

ACKNOWLEDGEMENTS

Thanks are due to the following for providing photographs, information or other assistance: Marion Beaton, John Cooper, Susan Doherty, Margaret Gray, Etta Kearney, Margaret McGrotty, Sheila Ogilvie, Netta Stewart, members of Pollokshaws Heritage, Gordon Sharp, Graham Shields, and Mr and Mrs Strang. Special thanks are due to Jim Clydesdale for reading the proofs and providing feedback; to John Howatt for allowing me to use the photographs from 1932; and George Smith for legwork (in his car!).

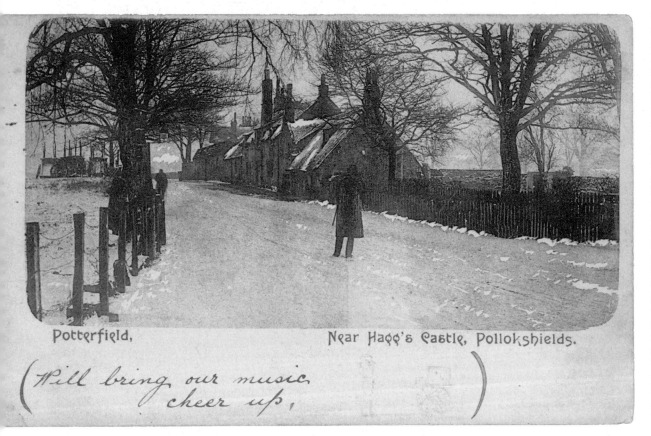

Potterfield, Near Hagg's Castle, Pollokshields.

(Will bring our music cheer up,)

Whins of Potterfield, seen here on a postcard sent in 1903, was the site of a pottery established in 1750. *Old Pollokshaws* also included a view of Whins of Potterfield, and this winter snow scene, initially thought to show the same location, came to light after its publication. In comparing the rows of houses in the two pictures it quickly became obvious that they were not the same, and a closer look at the 1858 Ordnance Survey map revealed that there were actually two rows of dwellings at Potterfield lying about a hundred yards apart. The track that later became Haggs Road passed through the gap between them, running in front of the east face of the north row (illustrated here), then at an angle past the west face of the south row. In the nineteenth century there were two coal mines near Potterfield: Quarry pit to the east and Titwood pit to the south-east, while Lochinch pit was about half a mile away to the north-west. The buildings comprising the tiny hamlet of Potterfield were demolished *c*.1905.

FOREWORD

This is a companion volume to *Old Pollokshaws*, published by Stenlake in 2002, and is made up of a new selection of pictures accompanied by new captions. The photographs in *Old Pollokshaws* were laid out as a walk round the old town beginning at Haggs Road, a format I've used again here as far as possible. As the introduction to the original book was fairly comprehensive, it seemed unnecessary to go over the same ground again, and instead I suggest that readers refer to this for a potted history. For details of how to obtain copies of *Old Pollokshaws*, along with information on Stenlake's full range of books, please see the inside back cover.

My editor at Stenlake Publishing has asked me to add a note of explanation. Throughout the book I refer to tenements by their height in storeys. In Glasgow, the ground floor of a tenement, often occupied by shops or businesses, is traditionally not counted – so a three-storey tenements as described in the following text is actually made up of ground floor shops and three storeys of flats above! The same logic applies to tenement of other heights.

Old Pollokshaws was very well received, and I hope this second volume of photographs will awaken more memories of life in the 'Shaws in years gone by.

Robert Jackson's grocery shop at 11 Harriet Street, seen here *c*.1910, is also visible on the right in the picture on page 19. Among the products in the window are a variety of brands of cocoa: Mazawattee, Rowntree's, Bournville (Cadbury's), Van Houten's, and Rova, an early name that soon disappeared. On the top shelf is a packet of Marshall's semolina and bottles of what look like spirits, indicating that this was probably a licenced grocer. The next shelf advertises Beattie's Celebrated Bread. This company also made biscuits, which is why in the television series 'Taggart' the original Chief Superintendent, Beattie, was known as 'the biscuit'. On the shelf marked Bilslands' Bread there is an impressive display of ham and bacon, with varieties labelled 'Finest Mild Cured', 'Finest Belfast Smoked', 'Finest Boiled Bacon', 'Finest Boiled Ham' and 'Finest Ayrshire Bacon'.

The triangular Wellgreen, edged by a pavement and railings and with a well or fountain on the green itself, has long been a feature of Pollokshaws. It is seen here *c.*1925 from Haggs Road, with about fifteen newly planted lime trees round its edge. In 2004 ten of these trees have survived the building of the first, then second, medical centres. The ornamental granite fountain, seen on page 37 of *Old Pollokshaws*, is not visible here so must have been installed after this picture was taken. The tenement on the left stands in the short street known as Wellgreen, called Wilson Street until *c.*1930. Behind and to its right is the Sir John Maxwell School, then in the distance the isolated two-close tenement in Bengal Street known as Orchard Place, with to its right the Burgh Halls. Beyond the railings to the right of the green, Ashtree Road, which isn't recorded on the 1913 Ordnance Survey map, looks as if it is newly laid out to run from what was then Barrhead Road to meet Factory Street at the rear of the Townshouse. At the near right-hand corner of the picture, beside the gas lamp standard, is the entrance to the goods station of the LMS Railway, with its sign projecting up from behind the sleeper fence. Also seen are several of the tall posts which supported the span wires that carried the power supply for the trams.

Pollokshaws Road at Bengal Street *c*.1955. The registration number on the small commercial vehicle, MGG 867, seen disappearing behind the leading tram, was issued in 1954. The tramcar is a Corporation Transport Department Mk II Coronation 'Cunarder', fleet number 1335, first used in 1950 and withdrawn in 1961. It is on the No. 25 service bound for Carnwadric. Behind it is one of the main production batch of this type of tram on the No. 14 service to Arden. 150 of the latter were put into service between the end of 1937 – in time for the Empire Exhibition in 1938 – and 1941. Prominently visible is the rope looping down from the roof at the forward end of the cars which was used by the conductor to pull the current collector over at the terminus. Between the two adverts on the left is the railway signal bracket carrying the main line and slow line up starter signals at the outlet (exit) from Pollokshaws goods yard. On the right is the burgh halls boundary wall with entrance and exit gates, the pillars of which were surmounted by ornate iron brackets which carried decorative lights. The section of this wall facing the main road, and the war memorial behind it carrying 300 names, was subsequently moved back on two occasions for road widening schemes. Behind the Christian Street nameplate beyond the tram stop flag on the lamp post is the building seen on the back cover.

The pictures on this double page spread show Pollokshaws Burgh Hall with different features of interest in the background. The building was commissioned by Sir John Stirling Maxwell at a cost of £20,000, and completed and gifted to the burgh for the use of local individuals and organisations in 1898. Its architect was Dr (later Sir) Robert Rowand Anderson. There are two halls, the larger of which can accommodate up to 1,000 and the smaller around 200, plus a number of anterooms. The smaller picture dates from c.1910 and in the left foreground, behind the fence (where Christian Street would be laid out later), Craigie's Park seems to be under cultivation. In the distance on the right is the three-storey tenement in King Street at Cogan Street. The lower, light-coloured building in front of the tenement is the Royal George, which stood opposite Pollokshaws West United Free Church. The burgh hall was closed by Glasgow City Council in the 1990s, but has since reopened and is now in the care of the Burgh Hall Trust.

The Sir John Maxwell School is on the right of this 1931 photograph with Crum Street passing between it and the burgh halls, and the chimney of the baths in Ashtree Road, built in 1928, seemingly sprouting from the rear of the halls.

Opposite: The land seen here on the far side of Pollokshaws Road was being used as a market garden by Ernest Pickwell & Son when this photograph was taken in 1931. Part of it was laid out as an orchard which benefited the local urchins who raided it regularly, although they had to be wary because the owner's house at 2060 Pollokshaws Road (seen on page 9) overlooked it. Pickwell also had lockups to let and sold petrol at the Shaw Bridge at the far end of this plot of land. The tenement on the far right is part of the block owned by the Co-op.

Celebrations at Pollok House in 1957 for the twenty-first birthday of John Maxwell Macdonald, who is standing in the foreground. His mother, Mrs Anne Maxwell Macdonald, is at the left-hand edge of the picture talking with the woman with the handbag. John senior, his father, is standing in the centre of the view in right profile, with Mrs Speedy of South Lodge in Barrhead Road just beyond him facing the camera. Seated in the foreground and wearing the hat is William Adam of Kennishead Farm. Behind him are Mr and Mrs Strang of Leggatstone Farm (Mrs Strang provided the photograph) and Mrs Ferguson of the first Bankhead Cottage at 2060 Pollokshaws Road. In view elsewhere are Mr White, factor, and Mr Pitcairn, architect, both of the estate. Also present are officials of the following sports organisations: Poloc Cricket and Tennis Club; Cartha and Bellahouston Athletic Clubs; Titwood Cricket Club; Pollok, Cowglen, and Haggs Castle Golf Clubs; and Pollokshaws, Bellahouston, and Newlands Bowling Clubs. *Image courtesy of The Herald & Evening Times Picture Archive.*

Construction of the old bridge over the River Cart in what later became Pollokshaws Road commenced in 1798, and this photograph probably dates from *c*.1930 when it was still called Barrhead Road. Pollokshaws West signal box is on the left, while the low brick 'howff' at the end of the railway bridge parapet is where oil for the signal lamps was stored. Mr Pickwell's house stands at the entrance to Pollok Estate.

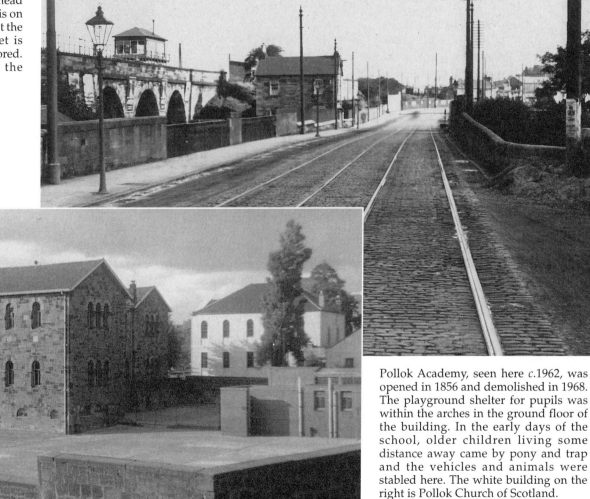

Pollok Academy, seen here *c*.1962, was opened in 1856 and demolished in 1968. The playground shelter for pupils was within the arches in the ground floor of the building. In the early days of the school, older children living some distance away came by pony and trap and the vehicles and animals were stabled here. The white building on the right is Pollok Church of Scotland.

Sadie Meldrum throws the first bowl of the season some time in the 1950s at Pollokshaws Bowling Club (founded 1854) on the club's green next to Pollokshaws Road, which is on the other side of the railings. This green occupied part of the ground between Afton Terrace and Pollok Academy. On the left is Sheeppark Lodge at the entrance to Sheeppark Farm Lane, framed by stone pillars. The 'on' single arm railway signal on the right-hand post was the 'down' Pollokshaws West station approaches stopping signal; the other post has the 'up' station starter and distant signals (the latter with fishtail arm) in the off position for Busby Junction. Note too the telegraph pole on the far side of the line carrying a large number of cables. These were once a feature of all railway lines and main roads. As a railway enthusiast I remember visiting Pollokshaws West signal box one morning in the 1960s having been attracted by unusual activity on the line. I found a chaotic scene with signalman John Gribben at his wits' end after thieves had stolen all the cables on both sides of this section of the line during the night for the copper, cutting communication between here and Busby Junction. The line was busier then because it carried a considerable amount of goods as well as passenger traffic, and as the section is on a curve with restricted visibility all movements had to be undertaken at walking pace until the cables were replaced.

This fine tenement of four closes in what was then called Barrhead Road is known as Afton Terrace. The Clydesdale Bank building in King Street, running parallel behind Barrhead Road, had a large garden at the rear that reached the four back courts of Afton Terrace, covering the same amount of ground as them. Beyond the tenement is the bowling green seen on the facing page with its tall white flagpole in profile against Pollok Academy. On the left, along the foot of the railway embankment, there were two villas plus other dwellings and business premises occupying the narrow strip of land between the railway station and Cunningham's garage at Pollokshaws West. Adjoining the garage there was a building containing two houses, next to which was the first Eastwood Parish Church hall. When a new hall was built next to the church in Mansewood Road around 1935, the old one was occupied by Walker's ham curing business. It remained there until the 1960s, then moved to a smaller building in Shawbridge Street, on the site of which there is now a children's nursery.

Pollokshaws West seen from the corner of Cross Street and Shawbridge Street, 1932. Kennishead Road, originally called High Cartcraigs, rises up on the left to cross the railway line, continuing on past the Greenknowe to Darnley and Barrhead. Note the police box and telephone kiosk at the tollhouse. Before the police had radios, police boxes were equipped with a blue lamp on the roof which flashed if a phone call came through for the patrol. In locations such as this one, the box might be out of sight of the patrol, so another light was set up in a more prominent position. Here the extension lamp can be seen projecting out at mid height from the nearest telegraph pole to the tollhouse. At the pavement edge to the right of the tollhouse is a pillar housing one of Glasgow Corporation Transport Department's emergency internal telephones. The smaller building with smoking chimney behind the tollhouse was a blacksmith's forge operated by Bryce Howatt. On the right is a bus emerging from Barrhead Road, possibly a Leyland Titan TD1 with Cowieson bodywork (and GG registration of 1929) that may have been on the No. 14 service running between Nitshill and Glassford Street in the city. The building on the right behind the garage is Low Cartcraigs, in one of the houses of which the popular political agitator John McLean lived with his mother for a time at the beginning of the twentieth century. The figure in the long white coat is a policeman directing traffic, known then as being on 'points duty'. There was not much for him to do in those days! The white foreshortened arcs above his head are the frontage of the two-bay private parking accommodation of Cunningham's Garage, which was built on the site of Mr Cunningham's blacksmith's forge. He had previously specialised in making gates and railings while Bryce Howatt mainly shod horses. The four white globes along the garage frontage are electric illuminated adverts for the Regent Petrol Company of a kind that were usually fixed on top of the (probably hand-cranked) pumps. The houses beyond the bridge, a single span then, were built for railway workers.

Two views looking north from different upstairs windows of a tenement in Kennishead Road around 11 a.m. on a summer's day in 1932. The train is probably on a local service to either Barrhead or East Kilbride. In the background of the right-hand picture the tower of the Burgh Hall and the chimney of the baths in Ashtree Road can be seen. Frame the carriers occupied the shed in the foreground of the left picture, with the open door situated at 36 Kennishead Road. Scott & Watson's soap and disinfectant works were nearby. Another of the buildings seen here is Bryce Howatt's stables, opposite the entrance of which, and out of sight apart from its shadow, is the two-storey tenement with Mrs Dean's sweetie shop at ground level. The upper floors of this tenement had a commanding view over Pollok Estate and the countryside to the west. Further down the hill, but unfortunately out of frame, there was an old villa which was known as the Black Boys' School. The term originated in the late eighteenth century when men from the West of Scotland, who went out to manage plantations in the Caribbean and prospered, sent their children back home to be educated. In this area too there was a vet's practice towards the end of the nineteenth century, and when the vet departed he left an articulated skeleton of a pony on the premises. It was still there when the building was being used as a dwelling, and in the 1940s an enterprising local lad used to charge children from outwith the district a ha'penny to view it.

The Round Toll *c*.1956, with Kennishead Road in the foreground and Cross Street to the left. The buildings in the background are, from the left, the original Methodist Church, the three-storey tenement containing Sandra Vetturini's cafe and the Mason's Arms pub at street level, the two-storey Jubilee Building with its twin gables in Cross Street, and another three-storey tenement, this one in Harriet Street at the corner of Nether Auldhouse Road. Note the washing line to the right of the tollhouse. Tenement dwellers hung their washing to dry in the back court, using a rope that was usually strung between four poles, giving up to six stretches of line on which to hang large loads. As wet clothes caused the rope to sag householders had one or two eight-foot long wooden clothes poles with a notch at one end for the rope. The other end was cut to a point so that it dug into the ground. Like the one seen here supporting a peculiar looking item of 'washing', these were used to prop up the line at the centre of a stretch.

When this old building in Cross Street at Kennishead Road was demolished in 1932 (the year the photograph was taken) it allowed the road to be widened. The ground floor premises with the 'Confections and Teas' sign was at one time a pub. Closely following the tramcar is a single deck bus, behind which is the low building (seen more clearly on p18) which was removed to allow Nether Auldhouse Road to be laid out, work on which was about to start at this date. Seen against this building are a coal merchant's cart and white horse. On the right are the public phone box and police box. The disembodied arm at the right-hand edge of the picture belongs to a policeman on points duty, sporting white pull-on sleeves instead of a white coat. The motorcycle combination parked at the box is probably his.

The two buildings at the left-hand end of this row – situated in Harriet Street between the Wellmeadow (now Sunlight) Laundry and Westwood Road – were demolished soon after this 1932 photograph was taken, and the two-storey red sandstone Corporation tenements in what is now Thornliebank Road at the corner of Westwood Road were put up in their place. The other buildings, including the shop at No. 74, lasted until the main redevelopment of Pollokshaws in the 1960s, and in 2004 this site is occupied by a grassy plot with advertising hoardings. The laundry premises were behind the buildings, with access provided on the right by the fence; unfortunately the sign on the gable end isn't legible here. Whilst dedicated poles were generally put up to carry the span wires for the trams, the lamp post on the near side of the road is also being used for this purpose here.

This row of buildings on the east side of Harriet Street stood opposite those on the facing page. The street numbers here are (from the left) 95 to 107. No. 105 was accessed at the rear through the passageway between the buildings. Behind the three-storey tenement on the left is Greenbank Park, from where the Auldhouse Burn was diverted to flow along its present route through Auldhouse Park to enter the River Cart above the weir. Originally it followed a winding course to the north, passing behind the Victoria Pottery and the end of Cogan Street before turning north-west under Shawbridge Street to run into the Cart close to the bridge in Pollokshaws Road. When the diversion was made in the late eighteenth century, the original course had to be retained as a mill lade to continue to supply existing industries that had been set up along its banks, and although the lade was last used in the 1920s the outflow into the Cart could still be seen as a trickle as late as the 1960s.

The low buildings in this 1932 view of Harriet Street are empty and ready for demolition. That's Alec Knox leaning on the saddle of his bike, with the arched entry to the pend in the centre of the picture leading to Clark's Close. Most houses in tenements in working-class areas, like the one seen here on the left, were comprised of two apartments with high (ten to fourteen foot) ceilings. They were known as 'room and kitchens' and were entered from the staircase landing by a main door that led into a (usually small) hall known as 'the lobby'. There was generally a shared toilet on the half-landing of the staircase. Each house had two tall, shallow cupboards, called 'presses', set into the walls with up to six shelves. All the doors in each house – outer, inner, and presses – were of solid wood with four recessed decorative panels, and were painted dark brown. Internal apartment doorknobs were incorporated in a metal plate which had a sliding locking device on the inside called a 'snib'. In a later age of home improvements, occupants took great delight in flush-panelling these doors with hardboard, but thirty years or more on, tastes changed again and new occupants removed the panels, once again appreciating the old-time design.

Harriet Street at Cross Street looking north, *c.*1900. James MacDougall, of the tailoring and clothing business seen here on the left, was the penultimate provost of Pollokshaws, serving from 1905 to 1911. The pub premises on the right, with the beer barrel suspended above the entrance, can be seen on page 20 of *Old Pollokshaws* at which time (*c.*1910) it bore the sign 'Fish Restaurant' (possibly a grandiose name for a chip shop). Beyond the tarpaulin-covered cart is the Y-shaped junction with King Street. James Pollok's dairy, referred to on the inside front cover, was on the right, opposite the cart which is parked outside what became known as the Jubilee Building.

In 1957, when this photograph was taken, Dr Ellis Glekin's surgery was at 287 Shawbridge Street, with Charles McClurg's fish and chip shop to its left at No. 285. Alf Vetturini's Glen Cafe was at No. 283, but is obscured here by the lower building which projected further into the street than its taller neighbour. The cafe was later managed by Alf's daughter Sandrina and became known as Sandra's Cafe. At No. 277 there was a pend, then the Mason's Arms pub at 273/275. The sign on the projecting gable of the low building beyond the tenement is advertising Willie Shannon's fruit shop at 271. From what can be seen of the motorcycle on the right outside the newsagent's at No. 291, it appears to be a BSA 500 cc twin cylinder. The car is a Morris, either an Oxford or a Cowley, with a 1954 Glasgow registration number, MYS 174.

Shawbridge Street looking north from in front of the Jubilee Building in 1957. On the left are the premises of funeral director Charles Freer at No. 316, with the driver of one of his cars, a Humber Snipe with a 1951 Glasgow registration number, JGE 749, looking out from the alleyway. The car on the left appears to be a post-war Standard 8. In 1957 I shared a second-hand 1939 model of this marque (CGE 864) with a friend, and clearly remember features including the running-boards on each side under the doors, the single tiny mirror fixed on top of the mudguard, and the side- and headlights farther forward. I also recall with horror the inefficient cable-operated brake system that had to be frequently stripped down, cleaned, greased, reassembled and adjusted. On the right is an Austin A35 with Dumfriesshire registration TSM 97. The even numbers in Shawbridge Street ended with the Methodist Church at 334, and the owner of Nos. 314–332 and 288 was the well-known eccentric millionaire of the middle years of the twentieth century, A. (Angus) E. Pickard. Beyond Freer's is Andrew Strang's ladies' outfitters and the branch of Galbraith's grocery store at No. 312 which was set up in opposition to the Co-op grocers not far away.

Shawbridge Street (called King Street until 1930/31) looking south, 1932. The premises of the Clydesdale Bank were at No. 268, but No. 270 also belonged to the bank and from its well-maintained appearance here it may have been the residence of the branch manager. In the 1950s the Clydesdale merged with the North of Scotland Bank and the titles were combined. The presence of seven chimneys on the gable next to the bank is puzzling; four of them would have belonged to the flues from the rooms of the house, but were the other three really for the bank? In the early 1950s I worked as a junior salesman in a busy Co-op grocery store in Pollok, the takings from which had to be carried to the nearest bank on a Friday, in this case the branch illustrated here. Along with three or four other junior staff, I took turns to take the money. Security was non-existent in those days, and it was a case of carrying around £600 (equivalent to about £10,000 today) on the bus(!) wrapped up in a paper poke. Captain Douglas Neale of the Salvation Army was one of the tenants of the tenement at No. 308 seen on the previous page. The tenement in the distance on the left contained the Jubilee Restaurant, which was owned by Boni Antinori, an Italian who was interned in 1940. He didn't reopen the restaurant after the war.

Shawbridge Street looking north towards Maxwell Cross, 1932. The viewpoints from which this photograph and the one on the facing page were taken are each visible in the other. The Clachan Bar at 248/252 Shawbridge Street occupied the three-storey building on the left beyond the Clydesdale Bank. Andrew McCallum, editor of the *Pollokshaws News*, was a familiar figure at this time walking daily from his house, Gowanbrae in Mansewood (originally Kirkhill) Road, to the Clachan, where he is reputed to have gathered most of his reportage. Beyond the pub, in the far distance, the old building known as the Royal George can be seen. Too bad the car on the right, the rear of which is seen opposite, isn't close enough to be identified, but it might be a 'Bullnose' Morris of the 1920s. At the end of the Second World War there was a vacant plot where the building in the right foreground is seen, on which a single prefab was built. This was occupied by a popular local woman, Mrs Law, for about fifteen years. Other prefabs were constructed in Maida Street, Ashtree Road and Tracy Street. Just out of frame on the right was a good quality single close two-storey red sandstone tenement at 229 Shawbridge Street, which was set well back from the pavement alignment of the adjacent low buildings.

The Victoria Pottery in Cogan Street was founded in 1855 by David Lockhart and Charles Arthur and continued in production under the Lockharts until the 1950s. It produced decorated tableware, jugs, bowls and ornaments, with the pottery stamp rendered as Pollockshaws rather than Pollokshaws prior to 1911. Some items can be seen in the People's Palace Museum on Glasgow Green, but none are found with a date-stamp later than 1911, after which it is believed the pottery concentrated on plain white ware. This group of workers was photographed *c*.1930.

Back row: Emma Hamilton, unknown, Peggy Bryden, unknown, Mary Nicol, Jessy McCabe, Jean Baird, May Dryden
Middle row: unknown, Maggie Wiseman, unknown, Mary Nicol, unknown, Anne Baird, Betty Knox, Kate Dryden
Front row: George Morton, Charles Madden, Tom Brierton, Johnie McKenna

King Street north of Maxwell Cross, *c*.1920. The white sign projecting from the close on the left is a 'Shop to Let' notice at what became 232 Shawbridge Street when the street name was changed. Beyond it a corner of the Royal George building can again be seen, while opposite is the Pollokshaws West United Free Church, with Auldfield Parish Church beyond. Among the shops in the three-storey tenement on the right is a grocery branch of the Pollokshaws Co-operative Society. In the 1950s there was a women's dress shop at No. 191 in the names of Jean and Catherine Williams, and another at No. 193 in the name of Susan Williams. The post office at No. 189 was in the name of Cecilia McWhirr, and Robert Clyde's grain store was at No. 185.

KING STREET, POLLOKSHAWS.

The building known as the Royal George, seen here in 1932, was reputed to have been constructed as a hotel early in the nineteenth century in the days of the stagecoaches, and is marked on the 1858 Ordnance Survey map at a time when these were the only form of public road transport, which seems to support the theory. It was probably converted to apartments before the turn of the twentieth century. The name may have derived from it being the terminus of a stagecoach service of that name between the city and the 'Shaws. I remember seeing it near the end of its life, when it was still occupied and in an extremely dilapidated state, but was never in it. Tales are recalled of squalid conditions towards the end, with leaking pipes and blocked toilets flooding passageways and plaster falling from the walls. In the 1959 Pollokshaws redevelopment compulsory purchase order, Compressor Services Ltd. are listed at 200 Shawbridge Street. The next address in the record is 212, this one, at which seventeen tenants are noted (near enough the capacity of the building). These were: Archibald Anderson, William Skinner, ____ Eastcroft, Marshal Scott, Francis McEwan, Henry Griffiths, James Scott, Lillias Babbs, Charles McLusky, George Pringle, John Donnelly, David Eastcroft, Ann McClusky, Thomas Rowantree, James Steven, George McAndrew, Archibald Keenan.

Shawbridge Street looking south from near the Shaw Bridge, 1932. The tree-bordered Shilling Ground, behind which two women with babes in arms are having a blether, is where in previous centuries Pollok Estate's tenant farmers winnowed their grain before it was ground in the laird's mill on the riverbank next to the bridge. It was a condition of tenancy that crops from estate farms be brought here to be milled. The process of winnowing grain involved tossing it up in the air in a breeze to allow the lighter husks to be blown out. In the middle distance the Royal George is framed in part by a mature tree, the gap probably having been opened by lopping to give headroom for road traffic. The shops in the distance, seen on page 25, have their sunblinds down. The building on the right was Pat McKenna's. Pat was a general dealer handling scrap material and second-hand items who sometimes operated on the margins of the law. His best-known escapade was when police found him in possession of a blacksmith's anvil, which he is reputed to have claimed he found floating down the River Cart! His more likely explanation was that it had been fly-tipped in the river.

In this 1932 picture Pat McKenna's building, with the King Street nameplate still visible, has been unroofed ready for demolition, after which the site was cleared for an expansion of John McDonald (Pneumatic Tools) Ltd. at 174–194 Shawbridge Street. The stone protrusion on the face of the building to the right of the nameplate may have been the gutter downpipe support of the adjacent demolished property located where the paling is seen. What looks like a doorway in the opened-up gable between these buildings was probably a shallow cupboard of the type described on page 18. McDonald had other premises at the riverside close to the bridge at 1 King Street (later 131 Shawbridge Street) probably on the site of the meal mill, where they tested the turbines they manufactured. In the background on the left is the rear of the Royal George building, while the smaller, nearer bungalow-type house was probably the office of Compressor Services Ltd. at 200 Shawbridge Street.

Standing opposite the Shilling Ground, the former Unionist Association Rooms building (seen here in 1932) may date from the era of the mill and could have been the miller's house. Today the Pollokshaws branch of the Grand Orange Order occupies the (extended) building. On the left are part of the premises of McDonald's turbine works, while in the space on the right Glasgow Corporation Cleansing Department later set up a depot at which Mr McAdam was the superintendent in the 1950s. The road or lane which leads off to the right here never had a name: all its occupants had King Street or Shawbridge Street addresses. It served a number of factories including the Greenholm Laundry, and that of Donaldson & Filer who made paper and cardboard in a red-brick building that was previously the Renfield Weaving Factory.

The old Shaws Brig, photographed in 1932 shortly before it was replaced by the present bridge. Note the chimney of the recently built (1928) baths and steamie in the left background. Behind the railings on the left, the houses at the riverside have been removed to make way for the increased width and shallower, more extended curve of the new bridge and road. The tenement in the left background is in Bengal Street at the corner of Bengal Place. The street nameplate on the gable in the centre of the photograph is that of Lilybank Place, which passed round behind the higher building, the Palladium Cinema, to meet Kirk Lane at its mid point. Previously the cinema was called the Maxwell, then during 1932 became the Palladium for a brief period before being renamed the Pollok. Part of the stone parapet of the original bridge seen here is still in place today next to the Orange Lodge, with the top of the coping at about waist height. This perspective of Glasgow Corporation Electricity Department's cast-iron street lighting fuse box, complete with coat of arms, gives a false impression of size; it actually stood about chest high. Of the buildings in Lilybank Place beyond the white-rendered gable with seven windows, one was 'an old smithy in what was known as Skin-mill Yard' according to the booklet celebrating the 125th anniversary of the Church of St Mary Immaculate. This goes on to explain that the former smithy was used as a Roman Catholic Chapel from 1850 to 1865, at which point the congregation transferred to the present building in Shawhill Road.

The weir on the River Cart seen from the Shaws Brig in 1932. The chimney and factory buildings belonged to Brown & Adam Ltd., cloth finishers and dyers, at their works in Factory Street. The building on the right had previously contained the meal mill sluice, the outflow from which is visible at bottom right. At this time the building, with its sluice, was used by John McDonald to test turbines.

Lilybank Place from the Shaws Brig, 1932. For a short distance, Lilybank Place followed the line of present-day Riverbank Street adjacent to the river, before turning to pass behind the Maxwell/Palladium cinema. This photograph and the one on the facing page bear a stamp reading 'Peter M'Cafferty, 1481 Pollokshaws Road, Glasgow, S.3, 30 August 1932' on the reverse, along with a handwritten note. The one accompanying this picture reads [*sic*]: 'An eighteenth century building which is now being demolished in terms of an order by the housing committee and for street improvements. The tennants of which have been accomadated in "Carnwadric Housing Scheme". A large part of this building was used as a forge by Mr James Muirhead until 1848 when he removed his business to Crossmyloof.' James Muirhead was the last member of the Muirhead family which, for over a hundred years, operated businesses in the area of Skin-mill Yard on the outside of the curve of Lilybank Place, where there is a plumber's business and car repair workshop in Riverbank Street today. A shammy [*sic*] mill for treating animal skins was started by the Tassie family here in the late seventeenth century, which gave the yard its name, and John Muirhead acquired half the business in 1752. The next operation was glue-making in season, then in 1830 James Muirhead set up the Cart Forge making axles for railway vehicles, before moving the operation to Crossmyloof. The tenement in the far background on the right is in Riverford Road at the entrance to the works of Brown & Adam Ltd.

Lilybank Place, 1932. Under the heading 'An Old Roman Catholic Chapel', the following contemporary notes accompany this print: 'The picture shows an old RC Chapel in Pollokshaws now being demolished. It was the first chapel in the burgh and came into being in the year 1850. The Rev Father Gallette, first resident priest in charge said mass in it until 1859, when a new chapel and school were built on Shawhill. There was a stone on the old building engraved with the letters AMDG which stand for Ad Majorem Die [sic] Gloriam (To the greater glory of God). This stone is now being preserved at the new chapel (Saint Mary's) on Shawhill.' The date of the closure of the chapel is not consistent with that quoted in the anniversary history of St Mary Immaculate. This picture and the one opposite are amongst about two dozen lent by John Howatt, but are the only two that are accompanied by a description. On the left is the partly demolished white-rendered gable with seven windows seen on pages 30 and 32, while the high brick wall on the right is that of the cinema.

The weir in the foreground was constructed towards the end of the eighteenth century to provide power for the meal mill, and at a later date the vacant mill site attracted John McDonald's works, which set up where the sluice could be used to test the turbines the company manufactured. This photograph dates from 1932, and these buildings were probably the original McDonald's premises in Pollokshaws, from which the company expanded to the site on the other side of Shawbridge Street (part of the frontage of which was where Pat McKenna's scrap business, seen on pages 27 and 28, was located). The flow of the river was concentrated here by the curve of the south bank, and water was made to run through the sluice to an outflow at a low wall that can still be seen in the river today. That wall is visible here below the south arch of the old Shaw Bridge, running from the sluice to the bridge pier. Above and to the left of this arch is the gable of Pat McKenna's building, the open rafters of which indicate that the roof is being dismantled. In the centre, projecting a little way above the chimney head of the tenement, is the short spire of Auldfield Parish Church (1837), while rising above the centre of the roof of the larger building on the left is the boiler chimney of the Greenholm Laundry situated behind the church.

Shawbridge Street looking north from the corner of Lilybank Place, 1932. The building on the left is being prepared for demolition to make way for construction of the new bridge, work on which took two years to complete. The faint FURNITURE BOUGHT sign projecting from above the nearest door seems to suggest that the establishment had been a second-hand store. Although there is nothing to indicate it, Pickwell's garage was at the rear of these premises, access to which was through the lane by the lamp standard. In the distance the sunblinds of the Co-op shops can be seen, and straight ahead the recently constructed baths and steamie are visible. The buildings on the right, adjacent to the three women, were also due for removal. The cinema, which opened in 1921, is set back out of sight on the right. Most main streets around the city were cobbled at this time, but while the rest of Shawbridge Street was subsequently resurfaced with tarmac the new bridge retained its cobbles until the 1960s.

Main Street (called Shawbridge Street from 1932) *c*.1910. The close on the left provided access to a billiards hall, as indicated by the sign outside. For a brief period before it was demolished in the early 1960s the hall was used, probably for rehearsals, by the Giffnock Theatre Players. Bengal Street is first on the left, on the far corner of which the Maxwell Arms pub was located. In the background is a bare gable with an empty fireplace from an apartment in a building demolished shortly beforehand. Sheltered housing was built on the vacant site between Bengal Street and Christian Street in 1983. The break in the pavement almost opposite Bengal Street, behind the black-clad figure of a man, marks the entrance to Kirk Lane.

Two women stand in the doorway of No. 5 Kirk Lane in 1932 while a cat sniffs around behind them. The taller building at the end of the row (No. 11) has a business sign projecting from it; in the 1950s plumber Donald Sime had a workshop here. Behind the post stopping vehicle access is the wall of the Old Vennel graveyard. Riverbank House, which stood next to the Viking Thread Mill, can be seen in the background. This house, situated at the dog-leg of the lane when it ran as far as Factory Street, became the residence of Mr Munn when he was caretaker of the mill. Note the long, narrow granite paving slabs laid at the horse-drawn cart iron-shod wheel spacing to reduce noise when the lane had through access. Such slabs were laid close to the pavement on busy cobbled main roads in certain places, and they really did cut down the noise of wheels, which particularly in the case of fast drivers could be almost as loud as that of the riveter's and boiler maker's pneumatic hammers. The well-known actor Alex Norton, currently starring in the STV series 'Taggart' as DCI Burke, lived here in the early 1960s.

The central premises of Pollokshaws Co-operative Society at 72–104 Main Street, seen c.1910 not long after they were built by the society around the turn of the century. The building had six shops at ground level with eighteen houses above these in three closes. Access to a small building used as a store by the grocery department was gained through the pend seen here beyond the last sunblind. John McNiven's Maxwell Arms pub stood at the corner of Bengal Street where the advertisement is seen painted on the wall.

The back court at 33 Main Street, seen in 1932.

The Townshouse, photographed in 1931, three years before the main part of the building was demolished leaving only the tower standing. Note the telephone box, and the gas lamp standard with the street name displayed across the top of the glass panel facing the camera. At one time it was fairly common for one or two lights along a street to be so-treated, with white letters on a blue strip (another example can be seen on page 25). The 'Fishmonger' sign on the left of the Townshouse indicates the original location of McClurg's fish shop, now located in the Stag building (named after the Old Stag pub which is out of sight behind the Townshouse), occupying the shop on the left next to the dairy.

The Townshouse, seen *c.*1900 from the raised section of pavement that ran along Pleasance Street between Shawhill Road and the police station (just out of sight on the right in the lower picture on page 42). Here, her head covered with what looks like a black patterned shawl, a woman is emerging from a back entrance to the last building on the nearer side of Shawhill Road. The three premises on the right had all changed hands by the time the lower photograph on page 42 was taken.

Photographed in 2000, this design of a cross within a circle, laid out in cobblestones on Greenview Street in front of the Townshouse, is reputed to mark the spot where the old Pollokshaws stone cross stood. Despite repairs and resurfacing the cobbles have been faithfully preserved for 120 years. The cross may have had to be moved when the tramline was installed in 1883, and when the road was laid with cobbles the design was painted on them. Efforts made in recent times to trace the whereabouts of the cross have been unsuccessful. One report was that it had been moved to Pollokshaws West but had subsequently disappeared. In a garden in Pollokshields there is a shaft on a stone base which at one time was topped with an ornamental ball. It could have been that at some stage the top of the Pollokshaws cross was knocked off and replaced with the ball, although it is not possible to say categorically that this is the missing landmark.

Although captioned 'The Square', this postcard actually shows Shawhill c.1910. The Square, located where the Townshouse stood, is out of shot to the left. The open area in the foreground here was formerly occupied by Pollokshaws gasworks, the site having been cleared after the turn of the century. The plant was closed when it was decided to take supplies from Glasgow Corporation's new Tradeston gasworks near Eglinton Toll. A pair of poles can be seen in Pleasance Street carrying the span wires supporting the overhead power supply cables for the single track tram line, while the low buildings on the left are at the foot of Shawhill Road. In a garden on the right some washing can be seen hanging out to dry. To the left of the drying clothes, the back wall of the pavement is higher than elsewhere and the chimney rising up from it indicates that the wash-house was here. The single-close tenement high up on the left was demolished soon after this time, and the 1913 Ordnance Survey map shows St Mary's Church hall standing on the site. Between this building and St Conval's Infant School, with its peaked roof above the staircase, part of the terrace of houses in Parkhill Road can be seen. Lower down, in line with the school and near the foot of Shawhill Road, is the entrance to the lane know as Dovecote.

The Square. Pollokshaws

Pupils at St Conval's Primary School, photographed in November 1946. The school was completed in 1926.

Back row: J. Connelly, J. McGhee, A. McGhee, T. Carrigan, J. Connelly, A. Narelli, J. Niblo, J. Broadly, P. Blair

Third row: J. McGhee, T. Fee, E. Bole, E. Hazlet, M. Harley, A. Riley, B. Morrison, M. Crawford, M. Cuthill, M. Bennett, G. Donaldson, C. Mullen, Miss McKee (teacher), T. Riley

Second row: M. Traynor, R. Hunter, J. Mulligan, E. Rossi, A. Mullen, E. Benntly, A. Wylie, A. Cannon, J. McKenna, A. Slapecus, J. McLaughlan

Front row: P. Harley, W. Martin, J. Ferguson, P. McMahon, A. McClymont, R. Farrell, N. O'Neil

Pollokshaws gasworks was established in 1836 on the site between McArthur Street and Pleasance Lane (then called Green Lane). Because of the upheaval caused by digging up roads to lay pipes, and the gas company's failure to restore road surfaces properly after work was completed, it had a strained relationship with the town council for much of its life. In 1846 street lighting was installed, then in 1891 Glasgow Corporation took over the works and continued to operate them until 1900. When the council's new plant at Tradeston became operational the supply was taken from there, and the Pollokshaws site was cleared and tidied up. It was later used for housing, with two tenement blocks put up on either side of McDougal Street, one close of one of which survives today at the corner of Riverford Road. This site at the corner of McDougal Street was also used for a fire station and a bathhouse. The latter occupied a small, low building constructed in 1909 by Glasgow Corporation with accommodation for six men and two women, which survives in McDougal Street in the space between the older building at the corner of Riverford Road and the newer red sandstone tenement.

This picture of the 'Toonshoose' dates from the late 1890s. Taken looking south-east, it shows the gas holder and chimney associated with the production plant in the background. Strangely, the tramline layout here does not conform with what is known about the system. The line was laid in 1883 by the Glasgow Tramcar Co. as an extension from Kilmarnock Road to a terminus in Main Street, ending in a run-round loop at the point where Christian Street was later to emerge. The extension along Greenview Street from this point to Pollokshaws Road was laid before 1900, but the original line turned off Greenview Street into Main Street here on the right, and survived to be shown on the 1913 OS map, although it is not visible in this picture.

Riverford Road in the 1930s showing the recently completed structure that replaced the old Baird's Bridge (seen on page 40 of *Old Pollokshaws*). During the 1930s the bridges over the River Cart at this location, in Pollokshaws Road and in Shawbridge Street (plus others along its course in the area and two or three over the Brock and Levern Burns) were all replaced by new, much wider structures with similar fine granite parapets. The Macquisten Bridge in Kilmarnock Road dates from 1907. At the extreme right-hand edge of the picture, a gate can just be seen in the railings leading to a set of steps. The gate provided access for workers at a cooperage and other factories situated on a lower level which was prone to occasional flooding. Until recently this area was very overgrown and jungle-like. However, the gate is still there, the greenery has been cleared and an effort is being made to provide a riverside walk all the way downstream from Linn Park.

Identification of this photograph has proved difficult. It was one of the series of views provided by John Howatt, but while all the others date from 1932 this one appears to have been taken earlier in the century. The tram line suggests that it is probably Pleasance Street, and these very old buildings may have been removed as part of the gasworks' site clearance. If so, red sandstone tenements were put up here by Glasgow Corporation in the 1930s. The 1913 Ordnance Survey map shows no buildings on this site (which was opposite the police station) at that date.

This is another of John Howatt's photographs that required a little detective work to identify. It was features on the three-storey tenement behind in Pollokshaws Road – mainly the pediment at roof level above the oriel windows – that helped place it. The buildings in the foreground are sited where the Corporation tenement was built in Pollokshaws Road in the late 1930s (now the location of Rossendale Court). At the time the photograph was taken a man known as Darkie McIntyre had a blacksmith's business in this vicinity, possibly in one of these buildings. Note the gap between the tenements in the background where there was a low building in which Willie Cassidy had a newsagent's (occupying the space at the bus stop where

there is now a passage into Mannering Court). Towards Haggs Road (to the left), electrical contractors Edgar & Mellan and Miss Miller's dairy occupied the three-storey building, and the Old Swan pub was further along at the corner of Haggs Road. It is recorded that 'during the second half of the nineteenth century, Peter Swan, a miner at Cowglen colliery, moved to Pollokshaws and became a spirit merchant' (*Born to Coal, The History of the Wingate Family, Part 1*, Dr Guy S. Wingate, 1992), and this is perhaps where the name of the pub came from.

Valuations of Farms of Pollok Estate

(Sir John Stirling-Maxwell Bart.)
By — Messrs Drennan & Scott

Name of Farm	Acres	Former Rent (£ s d)	Mr Drennan's Valuation	Mr Scott's Valuation
ARDEN	100	207 6 0	£190	£145
BURNFIELD	20½	51 13 0	45	35
BROOMPARK	127	227 10 0	190	150
BYRES	198	440 0 0	375	320
CARNWADRIC	186	460 0 0	382	345
CORKERHILL	160	311 3 0	280	235
COWGLEN	115	314 5 0	245	205
CATHCART MAINS	37	143 17 6	125	107
DEACONSBANK	105	87 16 0	80	70
DOVEHILL	107	280 0 0	260	210
DUMBRECK	7½	56 19 0	42	40
DARNLEY MILL	98	171 12 6	172	130
DARNLEY MAINS	253	522 13 0	410	320
DARNLEY (Upper)	110	165 0 0	145	120
HAGGSBOWS	117	308 13 0	245	180
HAGGSWOOD	14	71 14 0	40	37
HAUGH	108	218 12 0	190	175
HENRYSCROFT	56	137 10 0	110	105
KENNISHEAD	143	250 0 0	215	175
LOCHINCH	169	400 0 0	375	270
LEGGATSTON	85	115 10 0	105	90
MERRYLEE	162	360 0 0	324	275
NETHERTON	144	230 0 0	225	190
NETHER AULDHOUSE	118	213 0 0	213	160
PATTERTON	220	195 10 0	185	167
PAPERMILL	93	177 17 6	178	150
SHAWMOSS	240	489 12 6	400	325
SHEEP-PARK	183	513 6 0	412	340
SHAWBRIDGE HOLM	11½	60 0 0	55	43
WARDHILL	112	210 0 0	170	170
	3599	7391 0 0	£6383	£5284

This list of farms belonging to Pollok Estate was drawn up *c.*1910 when settling a rent dispute. The valuations of the estate manager, Mr Drennan, are compared with those of the arbiter for the tenant farmers, Mr Scott of Kelso. The buildings of eight of the farms listed still exist.